"Play, Learn, and Grow: Building Brains Together"

By Aaron Fields

Illustration By: Ayan Mansoori

ISBN: 978-1953-962-42-3

"Every moment spent together is a building block for a bright future". ------------Aaron Fields

A baby is born with a special gift—

A brain full of billions of tiny connections waiting to grow!

Even before they can talk, babies are busy!

They listen, look, and learn from you every day.

When you play together, you help build their brain,

Getting them ready for school, work, and all of life's adventures!

Look!

Children can use their eyes to gain knowledge.

What does your child like? What catches your little one's attention?

Talk about it together!

Attach!

Connect with your child—

Share a smile, a chat, a hug, and make funny faces!

Speak!

Your words make their brains light up!

Talk about your day, the yummy foods you eat,

Or make silly sounds together for fun!

Follow!

Children learn best when you join in their play and follow their lead.

Listen to their words, sounds, and watch their movements.

Then respond with your own fun ideas!

Take Turns!

Learning can be a game of sharing!

Taking turns when you're playing, talking, and exploring is important.

Expand!

Help your child's brain grow strong!

Keep the conversation going—

Ask questions that start with what, when, where, how, or why!

Even though you're busy, always make time for your child.

Building a healthy brain helps them learn important life skills,

Like self-control, focus, problem-solving, and facing challenges.

So let's learn together, every day,

And watch your child's amazing brain grow!

Nurturing the future of your child

Supportive and positive interactions with adults help the child's brain develop in a strong and flexible way. It's best to start building the child's brain from birth. Engaging in back-and-forth conversations with your child helps their brain grow. By doing this, you are shaping their mind and supporting their health, learning, and behavior now and in the future.

Ways To Promote Brain Development:

1. Creating a Healthy Environment for Children:

- Ensure that children have access to a safe, clean, and stimulating environment. This includes providing age-appropriate toys, books, and activities that encourage exploration and learning.

2. Positive Experiences:

- Help children participate in activities that foster joy, creativity, and curiosity. Positive experiences, such as playtime, storytelling, and music, can enhance cognitive development and emotional well-being.

3. Attachment:

- Promote secure attachments by being responsive to a child's needs. Being consistent with love and attention for the child can build a strong foundation for emotional and social development.

4. Neglect and Abuse:

- PLEASE understand that neglect and abuse can severely hinder brain development. It is essential to provide a nurturing environment free from harm, as adverse experiences can lead to long-term developmental challenges, especially when the child reaches adulthood.

5. Household Dynamics:

- Create a supportive household where open communication and encouragement are prioritized. Having a positive family atmosphere helps promote healthy brain development and emotional resilience.

6. Creating Strong Relationships:

- Encourage strong relationships with family members and peers. Social interactions are vital for developing communication skills and emotional intelligence.

Activities That Can Help Promote Brain Development

- **Reading Together:** Share/read stories together to enhance language skills and imagination.

- **Creative Play:** Arts and crafts can help stimulate creativity and fine motor skills.

- **Outdoor Exploration:** Believe it or not, spending time in nature can help promote curiosity and physical activity.

- **Music and Movement:** Introduce songs and dance to develop rhythm, coordination, auditory skills, and confidence.

- **Puzzles and Games:** Use age-appropriate puzzles and games to promote teamwork, problem-solving and critical thinking.

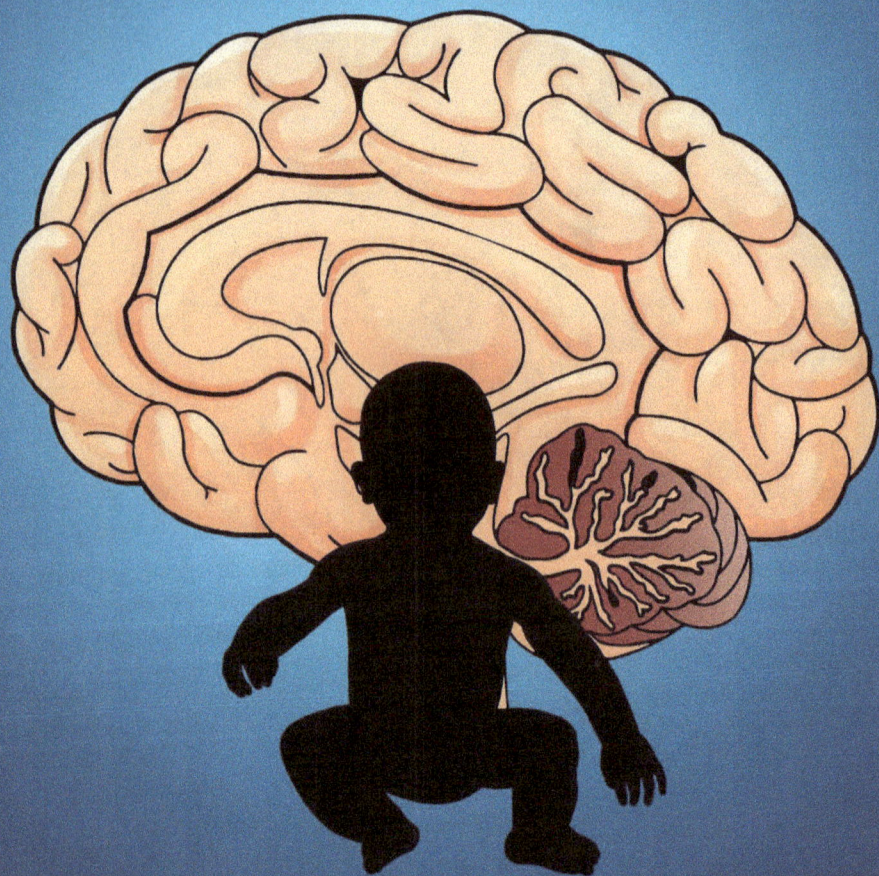

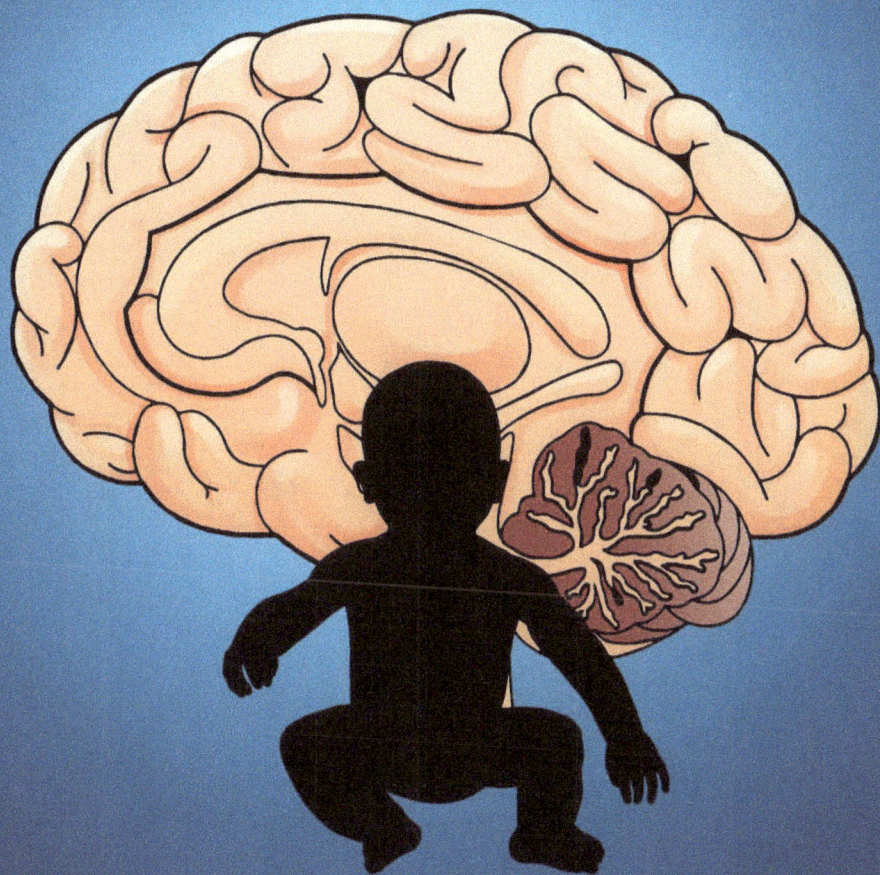

www.ingramcontent.com/pod-product-compliance
Lightning Source LLC
Chambersburg PA
CBHW081639040426

42449CB00014B/3386